Endorsements

This moving and eloquent collection of prose and poetry is a testament to the desire and ability of ordinary Irish people to express solidarity with Ukraine's suffering as a result of a Russian fascist invasion. Those who forget history are condemned to repeat it. The people represented in this admirable anthology have not forgotten.

CATRIONA CROWE – Archivist and Broadcaster

A welcome collection of insightful and moving thoughts; prose, poetry and reportage, from selfless and committed people who are out there, day after day doing something (to borrow a phrase from one of the pieces) at a time when it is important to act, make your voice heard, agitate, rather than sit back and watch events unfold and get worse.

AIDAN GILLEN – Actor

In Ireland we love the underdog. The reason is that for a very long time we were the underdog. We know what it is to be bullied and we know what it is to resist. We stood up against a great empire just as Ukraine is doing now. I am really heartened by the great humanity, compassion and concern displayed by the contributors to this anthology. It represents

a powerful expression of Ireland's solidarity with Ukraine and its people.
PETER SHERIDAN – Playwright, Director and Author

WE STAND WITH UKRAINE

WE STAND WITH UKRAINE

An anthology of Poetry, Prose and Protest

Edited by

JOHN FARRELLY, HELEN DWYER AND JULIAN VIGNOLES

MERCIER PRESS

MERCIER PRESS

www.mercierpress.ie

© Individual Contributors, 2023

ISBN: 978-1-78117-835-5

978-1-78117-836-2 (Ebook)

A CIP record for this title is available from the British Library.

Printed and bound in the EU.

Contents

This anthology is dedicated to the people of Ukraine for their heroic courage and resistance in the face of Russian aggression and to President Volodymyr Zelenskyy for his unflinching and unshakeable leadership of his country and people.

The anthology also recognises and remembers the many victims of this war:

The Bereaved
The Displaced
The Dispossessed
The Maimed
The Missing
The Murdered
The Raped
The Survivors
The Tortured
The Trafficked
The Traumatised
The Wounded
Slava Ukraini!

INTRODUCTION

The full-scale Russian invasion of Ukraine in February 2022 was a very significant moment in European history. Throughout the world, Russian embassies became the locus and focus of protest and demonstration. The Russian embassy in Dublin was no different. Large crowds gathered outside to chant and shout opposition to Russia's criminal and unprovoked invasion.

Though the protests in Ireland declined in size, a small group of protesters maintained their presence outside the Russian embassy compound on Orwell Road, Dublin 14. The group of up to fifty individuals from diverse backgrounds continue to demonstrate and hold aloft the blue and yellow flag of Ukraine.

After some months, an idea emerged to compile an anthology of written reflections by group members, to try and capture their individual motivations for the continued protest. It would hopefully, like the protest itself, act as support to Ukraine and its people in their struggle against Putin's regime, and also support Russian people protesting against the war, those who know the invasion is unjust but cannot speak the truth.

While some on the protest declined to contribute for personal reasons, this anthology contains prose and verse from thirty-four group members, written at various stages since the full-scale invasion began, the contributors preferring to use only their first names. One of the group, Declan Reid, has documented the protest with a camera and most of the photographs reproduced here are his.

We, the editors, are grateful to Mary Feehan and all at Mercier Press. All royalties from the sale of the anthology will be donated to Ukrainian Action, a not-for-profit organisation registered in Ireland (CRO #718898), whose aim is to help Ukrainians in need and foster Irish-Ukrainian friendship.

The residents of Orwell Road are deserving of acknowledgement for their understanding and tolerance of the presence of the protesters. Similarly, we acknowledge the professional manner in which gardaí have conducted themselves while on duty outside the embassy, having regard to the, at times, fraught and emotional nature of the protest.

JOHN FARRELLY, HELEN DWYER
and JULIAN VIGNOLES

Foreword

I am struck by the empathy, understanding and genuine concern for Ukraine and its people displayed in the individual pieces of poetry and prose contained in this anthology. Ukraine is at a critical juncture in its history and the support and understanding of free citizens throughout the world is very much needed and appreciated. I commend the core group of protesters for compiling *We Stand with Ukraine* and for continuing their protest outside the embassy of the Russian Federation on Orwell Road, Dublin 14.

The protest has been ongoing since the invasion began and is undertaken by a core group of very committed Irish citizens and residents. *We Stand with Ukraine – An anthology of Poetry, Prose and Protest* captures in very graphic and personal ways the motivations, feelings and thoughts of the members of the protesting group.

The criminal and illegal full-scale invasion of Ukraine by the Russian Federation, on 24 February 2022, marks a pivotal moment in the struggle between the forces of autocracy and the forces of democracy. The transgression of Ukraine's sovereignty and independence by the military machine of Vladimir Putin's regime provoked heart-felt sympathy and support for Ukraine and its beleaguered people. The proffered sympathy and support took many forms: sanctions against the Russian Federation, the supplying of arms and military equipment to Ukraine, the offer of accommodation to Ukrainian families fleeing the war, humanitarian and medical aid. In many countries people raised their voices in condemnation of the invasion of Ukraine and demonstrated publicly against the illegal act. In Ireland demonstrations and protests were held with many thousands of people in attendance.

I recommend this anthology to anyone interested in or concerned about democracy, justice, and the right to demonstrate and protest. On my own behalf and on behalf of all Ukrainians, especially the Ukrainian community in Ireland, I salute the committed band of protesters who continue to freely demonstrate on Orwell Road.

GERASKO LARYSA
AMBASSADOR EXTRAORDINARY AND
PLENIPOTENTIARY OF UKRAINE TO IRELAND

SEASONS – ORWELL ROAD

Barry (pacifist)

I've watched green leaves sprout
Turn yellow, brown and fall
Wind rain, sun and all

Cars, people, dogs and bikes
Smiles, waves, fingers and beeps
Still this senseless war rages on

Bearing Witness

Terry (retired public servant)

My late mother was born on 24 February. Every year, on that day, I bring the first of the spring planters to my parents' and grandparents' graves. This was the plan for 24 February 2022. Then I heard the 6 a.m. news on RTÉ radio and cried for the people of Ukraine. I made coffee and wrote to the Ukrainian embassy expressing my sorrow and support. I was definitely in shock.

I did put the flowers on the graves that day. And I cried again, not for the loss of my parents, but for the people of Ukraine. It was a grey, cold, drizzly day. Later, I walked up to the Russian embassy, a place I have passed on walks for thirty years. There were people standing around outside. Sad, shocked and fearful people. I stood with them.

I went up to the embassy repeatedly and found myself standing outside it with a band of people. I crocheted a Ukrainian flag and placed it in my porch.

I placed the yellow and blue ribbon on my coat; it's still there. I repeatedly asked fellow protesters 'How will this all end?' I had to stop watching the news because it affected an already bad sleep pattern. The constant theme of conversations outside the embassy was 'there is so little we can do, but we have to do something'.

More than twelve months on and I still stand outside the Russian embassy. In my case, I stand in silence. I stand with a simple blue and yellow flag. I stand in witness for the atrocities committed by the Russians against the women and children, old, disabled, sick people and also animals. There is little else I can do. I donate but I believe protest is necessary. My way of protesting is silent. I am not a by-stander. I am a witness.

When I walk up the road, I feel relieved to find other like-minded people are still there, protesting, witnessing. I will continue for as long as I have the health and strength to do it. I pray for peace but know that Putin cannot be trusted and I leave resolution to the Ukrainian people, whose blood has been shed in defence of their sovereign, democratic state.

The Voice

Brendan (Rathgar resident, sportsman, engineer)

Six months into Russia's war on Ukraine, standing alone outside the embassy of the Russian Federation, holding a Ukrainian flag as the city awakes, and thoughts turn to the feelings of a runner on his or her maiden marathon.

No sign of the finish line. Will I get there? Is this pace OK? This seems to be going on forever. Am I putting in enough effort, or too much? Is this crazy? How will I feel if I stick it out to the end? Will it be worthwhile when it's over?

The runner is encouraged along the way by small acts and gestures and the spirits are lifted. It may be a smile, a clap, a familiar face, a kind word of encouragement or the old lady handing out Starburst sweets. The small gestures answer the inner doubts and the finish line appears achievable. Stopping is not an option. The effort will be worthwhile.

Cars pass by. Pedestrians and cyclists pass by. The occasional runner. People lost in their thoughts of a busy day ahead. The blue and yellow flag catches the attention of some, and brings their thoughts momentarily to a very different place where democracy is brutally assaulted by an evil tyranny. Awareness restored; important not to forget.

A large figure approaches. A friendly face. Bright eyes. Then a Voice starts speaking in an unfamiliar language – Ukrainian? Russian? Maybe. Who knows? Realising that the flag-bearer is just a local person of no importance, the eyes light up and the Voice begins to speak in English. Just then the interaction is interrupted by the gatekeeper at the Consular Department, who invites the Voice to enter.

Back to quiet contemplation, interrupted only by a few individuals passing through the gate to the Consular Department, silently passing by the Ukrainian flag. A few cars with 'CD' registration plates enter the gates of the embassy. Each 'diplomat' being obliged to drive beneath the flag of a nation that their president refers to as a historical mistake of the communists.*

Business concluded at the Consular Department, the Voice re-emerges and pauses. This time the eyes look serious and intense. In a quiet, slow and deliberate tone the Voice says: 'Thank you. What you are doing here is very important'.

With that, the Voice drifts away into the morning, but the words 'Thank you. What you are doing here is very important' linger in the air and remain as a permanent fixture at the embassy gates. Any inner doubts are answered. The finish line may not be visible, but the effort to get there will be worthwhile.

* *New York Times*, 21 February 2022, article by Michael Schwirtz, Maria Varenikova and Rick Gladstone.

On Orwell Road

Richard (retired systems administrator)

Busy parents pushing prams
Young lovers holding hands
Dog walkers on their daily stroll
Children on their way to school
We could happily watch the world go by
No heavy hearts, no need to cry
But cry we must and shout and scream
While people die for a tyrant's dream
A people led by lies and might
A people dying to defend their right

Flares light up the fields of wheat
Families cower and animals bleat
The nuclear threat a blip away
A red button a world under sway
We can only watch and be aware
Pray with hope, switch off despair
The young live life no time for fear
Distant drums it could not happen here
We see the danger life taught the code
We stand against war on Orwell Road.

History Repeating Itself

Maarten (semi-retired university professor)

As soon as the threat by Russia against Ukraine started, the beginning of the Second World War came to mind. The same situation exists now, whereby a large, powerful, country and its leader set their eye on a neighbour with whom there are long-established historical and cultural links. In both cases, a megalomaniacal despot brainwashed their citizens into believing the righteousness of their planned war and conquest. In Hitler's case, it was the idea of Lebensraum and the Untermensch, with Putin it is a nostalgia for the old Tsarist (serf-based) empire and the past greatness of Russia.

I had believed all my life that the horrors of the Second World War would prevent any recurrence of war and invasion in Europe, especially by what was the former Soviet Union, which lost more than twenty-five million people during that war. But apparently,

Putin's delusional dream of recreating a Greater Russia allows him to send his troops into Ukraine without any justification, where they are committing war crimes on a massive scale and where many Russian soldiers are dying without really knowing what for.

I grew up in the Netherlands, where I was born only eight years after the end of the Second World War. Both my parents had experienced the horrors of war. My father spent several years in a prisoner of war camp in occupied Poland; my mother was a nurse in Amsterdam caring for many starving and sick people. The winter of 1944–45 is known in the Netherlands as 'the hunger winter', when thousands of people starved to death because the German occupiers had requisitioned most available food. Many people in the big cities walked far into the countryside to try to barter any household goods for whatever food they could get their hands on.

These memories of my parents' experiences and the destruction and suffering that war brings were brought back vividly by the images coming out of Ukraine of bombed houses, apartment blocks and hospitals, and of people dying or fleeing for their lives, losing everything. The total disregard by the Russian army for civilians, by targeting cities and residential areas with rockets and artillery, killing many children and women, reminds me of the slaughter in eastern Europe and Russia by the German army. According to Putin, the Ukrainian and Russian peoples are very closely related, if not actually one people, and the purpose of the war is supposedly the de-Nazification of Ukraine. But the actions carried out in his name show a total disregard for the Ukrainian people, and indirectly, for his own.

This family connection with the evils that war brings made me decide to go to the Russian embassy to express my opposition to the invasion and the crimes being committed by the country and ruler that they represent.

I feel proud standing there holding my Ukrainian flag high and letting the ambassador and his lackeys know what I think of their country's crimes and their presence in Ireland. It would be great if Russia realises the error of its ways and ends the war by withdrawing from Ukraine. But until that time, I will continue to join the other protesters as often as I can.

Paws for Thought

Molly (on behalf of Siobhán – retired public servant)

My name is Molly. I am a six-year-old Collie/Belgian Shepherd cross dog. I am the founding member, chief executive and President of Paws Against Putin. My human has always belonged to various protest groups but this is all new to me.

Back in March 2022 I started coming to protest Russia's invasion of Ukraine. As a rescue dog, I can be very nervous of new situations, places and noises. I was very anxious at first when supporters tooted their horns passing the protesters. Now I present a relaxed, serene front for all to see. My human thinks it's important to show up lest the world begins to forget the daily suffering of the people of Ukraine.

I would love more dogs to join me outside the embassy. All are welcome but remember I'm still the boss.

Over my Garden Wall

Joan (local resident)

Over my garden wall it is 'Russian soil'. It is that close to me the Russian embassy, its inhabitants privileged and protected by 'Diplomatic Immunity', which gives cover to these agents of death and destruction to continue their genocide and crimes against humanity – spies, liars, experts in propaganda.

It is midnight, a beautiful full moon shines down and I open the blind on my kitchen window. All is silent; the daily group of protesters have long since gone home, the chanting of 'Shame on you' and the honking of car horns has died away. An eerie quiet reigns.

These privileged and protected people are sleeping in their beds, resting and dreaming up more lies and plans for atrocities and propaganda to justify their evil deeds to the world.

How can this be right? I am overcome

by a feeling of despair and helplessness. My thoughts then turn to the proud and patriotic Ukrainian people whose courage and indomitable spirit of endurance will not be broken. We must believe that their determination to achieve independence, freedom and justice will not wane and that those who have paid the ultimate price by giving their lives for their country will not have died in vain, that they will be free.

Under a moonlit sky at midnight, looking over the wall into 'Russian soil' I say to you Vladimir Putin, Yuri Filatov and all your spies and agents of death and destruction:

Shame on You All.

Slava Ukraini!

To a Russian Soldier

Helen D (retired public servant)

When you are close to death
Either tomorrow on the field of war
Or years away when you are old –
You will remember.

You will remember the look of revulsion
In her dark blue eyes,
The woman you locked in a potato cellar
And raped until you shot her in the head,
And left her there wearing a fur coat
And nothing else.

You were able to take her body
But you couldn't take her mind.

And you will see her
For the rest of your life
Every time you close your eyes.

You will remember the little girl

You shot in the back as she fled
Screaming in Mariupol.
You will remember the blood
On her blonde curls
As she lay on the ground
And you targeted another child.

You will remember those children
Every time you close your eyes.

You will remember the landmines
You planted in golden fields of corn.

You will remember the babies
Murdered before they were born.

And you will wonder
As long as you live
What was it all for?

Frost People

Dymphna (retired teacher)

The film footage is silent, sombre and deathly impending. The scene is dark. A young woman is seated with her back against a wall. She is holding a small child on her lap. She raises her right arm and sweeps her face. We can hear her silently weeping. Her child is calm. He may be asleep – or tired – or bewildered. We cannot tell – his face is downward and turned away from the camera.

She doesn't appear to have any belongings or indeed anything at all at her side, apart from the treasure on her lap. She is not alone. Other people are moving around her in the darkness. I assume that she is another civilian casualty from a sudden and violent invasion and has lost her home and all her belongings from yet another shelling. But this particular picture fails to 'paint a thousand words'. Words are necessary here and we are eventually told that she has lost an even younger child to the shelling overhead and was forced to flee to this place with her remaining living child who has become her sole reason for survival.

In all my years I have never seen a scene as hopeless, helpless and despairing as this. In my mind I have called her Maria and I have already established a strong emotional link with her and it is not just because I am a mother or because she could be my daughter – it is because I am a human being and my occasional presence outside the Russian embassy in Dublin is purely in empathy with Maria and all those that she has become a symbol of.

I do not carry hatred in my heart when I stand outside the embassy. I carry thoughts of Maria. I think of her every day while I live the banalities of everyday life which I have come to think of as a privilege, a privilege that has been denied to a young woman who is being punished mercilessly to the end of her days for the sin of being innocent.

I ask myself 'How is she? 'How is her living child? 'Where is his father?' 'Where is she now?' I know in my heart that no matter how kind people may be to her, even if she has been provided with safe sanctuary for the rest of her life it will not fill the gaping hole in her heart. I imagine that every day she walks around a deep, dark chasm of loss that she just wants to throw herself into but cannot because she has another life besides her own that she is responsible for. It may help that sometime in the future she may be reunited with the remains of her youngest child and she may be able to grieve and honour him. The improbability of this small ask is what encourages me personally to continue to stand opposite the embassy which represents those who have done all this to her.

I stand with people who have their own personal reasons for being there. We did not know each other before the invasion and we may have different approaches to those entering and leaving the embassy but my own instincts have told me that these people who stand there on a regular basis have empathy at their core and I am proud to stand with them. We try not to use offensive language or gestures. I cannot say that we never did but I can say that we generally don't and we would not encourage it among people who join us. We have come to know that offence doesn't serve us – and it doesn't serve people like Maria, so while some of us coldly greet vehicles entering and leaving the embassy chanting how unwelcome they are we do so without letting ourselves or Maria down.

We are the people that Mr Yuri Filatov (the Russian ambassador to Ireland) has referred to as 'Frost People'. This term is used to define people who operate outside of the law. The phrase is further defined as 'Thugs'.

Maria – I don't know where you and your child are but I will stand for you and for all those who are suffering like you through this sudden, cruel, unprovoked and unnecessary war and I hope that the words of our own Terence MacSwiney may help you all through this time.

> It is not those who can inflict the most but those who can suffer the most who will conquer.

Easter 2022: Russian Embassy Staff Seek Some Heat

John F (retired community worker, educator and researcher)

(Due to lack of oil for the central heating system, staff in the Russian embassy in Dublin complained of the cold):

Heat yourselves by the red fanned fires of
    Bucha, Kharkiv and Kherson
Heat yourselves by the cremated bodies of
    Mariupol's innocent civilians
Heat yourselves by the hot air and lies of
    Putin and his lackey Lavrov
Heat yourselves by the fetid breath of all the
    Kremlin's lapdogs
Heat yourselves by the sirens loud wailing
    screeching screams
Heat yourselves by the collapsing flats and
    caved in domestic beams
Heat yourselves by the bullet strewn cars and
    twisted armoured wrecks

Heat yourselves by the lifeless bodies at street
corners and roadside checks
Heat yourselves by the jet streams of your
military's murderous mission
Heat yourselves by the cowardice of your
president's political position
Heat yourselves by the cowering crowds in
subways and bomb shelters
Heat yourselves by the inhumanity manifested
in a hell like smelter

Heat yourselves by the fleeing children's lost
eyes and tepid tears
Heat yourselves by the weeping mothers and
fathers' frozen fears
Heat yourselves by the televised images of
war, agony, and despair
Heat yourselves by the ghostly streets with
the absence of people there
Heat yourselves by the lethal clusters of
thermobarbaric bombs
Heat yourselves by the sight of decapitations
and shattered limbs
Heat yourselves by the remote accuracy of a
craven cruise missile

Heat yourselves by the policies from which
you refuse to resile

Heat yourselves by the burnt-out hospitals,
nurseries and schools

Heat yourselves by the utterances of blind
idiots and useless fools

Heat yourselves by the light of a free and un-
censored media

Heat yourselves by the foregoing of your
excuses and apologia

Heat yourselves by confronting the daily
deathly explosive truth

Heat yourselves by eyeing mouths left with
not a single tooth

Heat yourselves by seeing the brutality of
your leader's ardour

Heat yourselves by facing his narcissistic,
ruthless anger

Heat yourselves by reflecting on true facts in
the bathroom mirror

Heat yourselves by viewing a 'special military
operation's' squalor

Heat yourselves by feeling the fury and dis-
belief of world opinion

Heat yourselves by knowing you will never achieve your dominion

Heat yourselves by embracing the flag of the yellow and blue

Heat yourselves by grasping the sunflower's bright and radiant hue

Heat yourselves by the glowing globes of Kyiv's golden steeples

Heat yourselves by the heroics of an independent Ukrainian people

Hate yourselves for the hellish holocaust that you have commenced

Hate yourselves for the dystopia you have so coldly advanced

Hate yourselves for the war crimes you have certainly committed

Hate yourselves for the sly cynical lies told but never admitted

Hate yourselves for the barbarism and all the vicious fascist acts

Hate yourselves for the fake news and fraudulent false facts

Hate yourselves for the callous death, destruction, and despair

Hate yourselves for the shame, guilt, blame
    you will forever bear
Target the heat on your hate, apologise, with-
    draw, and truly liberate.

It Affects Me

Declan (retired company manager, old age pensioner and free Irish citizen)

I cannot un-see the television images. The horror and inhumanity of a senseless war ordered by an insane, tyrannical, powerful dictator who believes he has the right to annihilate a country and exterminate its people simply because he believes they should not exist.

It affects me.

The elderly lady in the wheelchair being carried across a narrow makeshift single walkway over a river with its destroyed bridge. Part of a long line of people, families, their lives in suitcases or plastic carrier bags, desperately fleeing the bombs and horror of war and not understanding why it is happening.

I sit in my house, safe and warm and I can see all this in real time on my television. A little Ukrainian girl, seven years of age, singing 'Let it Go' to cheer up distraught and fearful neighbours in an underground Kyiv bomb shelter.

It affects me.

Broken, twisted, bloodied little bodies, not moving, lying in the rubble of bombed apartments, hospitals, schools and playgrounds. The innocent victims of unguided munitions and deliberate targeted shelling.

Their young lives violently extinguished, their families fragmented – all at the pull of a lever on a Russian weapon of destruction from a safe distance, miles away or from the push of a remote button two decks down in a Russian ship on the Black Sea. The air raid sirens sound, and death comes indiscriminately from the sky. Genocide.

It affects me.

But there are other ways to unleash the terror. Russian soldiers in Irpin see the family running. A woman and two small children, a boy and a girl. They are no threat and have no weapons. They are simply terrified and running for their lives. The Russians bring their rifles up, maybe their semi-automatic AK-74s that have a muzzle velocity of two thousand nine hundred feet per second and a rate of fire in bursts of one hundred rounds a minute. They pull their triggers …

In Bucha, as they retreat, Russian forces simply leave murdered civilians on the streets, hands bound behind their backs, a signature for all democratic countries to see – the price of resistance and freedom.

It affects me.

On and on it goes – indiscriminate bombing, the levelling of beautiful historical cities, rape, murder, the forced migration of millions of Ukrainian women and children maybe never to see their husbands and fathers alive again. The cold, unemotional and insane planning to exterminate a free democratic peaceful country; Bucha, Chernihiv, Irpin, Izyum, Kharkiv, Kherson, Kramatorsk, Mariupol, Severodonetsk, Sloviansk. It's barbaric. The anguish of Ukraine and the world cries out for justice.

It affects me.

What can I do? Unlike the people in Russia who object to this unjust war, I can use my own constitutional rights under the freedom of my country's constitution and the European Court of Human Rights. I can come here to the Russian embassy in Dublin and be a small voice for Ukraine and humanity addressing the representatives, so-called diplomats, of this evil Russian regime and denounce its hateful vile actions against the free world. Ukraine must endure to be free again. We are witnesses. We will remember.

Slava Ukraini! Beir bua agus beannacht.

Ripples and Ribbons

Fidelma (retired)

The great tragedy of war is the number of people needlessly killed; the ripples of pain and trauma that spread through the community from each death will last longer than the war itself.

I wanted in some way to recognise the importance of each individual lost in this conflict by tying a ribbon for each one.

Sadly, there are too many now to keep up, but the ribbons are there to remind us that each death matters and many suffer because of each one.

THE POWER OF BLUE AND YELLOW

Julian (author and former RTÉ radio and television producer)

It's simple gesture: I hold a well-worn placard with Ukraine's colours and a message of solidarity. It's tattered now because Russia's evil persists. But I still stand with others – my friends now – outside the five-acre compound, the place that represents Putin's regime.

I think of the flag's blue – and those skies over Ukraine lit so often by the terror of the Kremlin's missiles. But yellow makes me remember the vast tracts of ripening grain that should be swaying peacefully. And I think of the disrupted harvest.

Embassy personnel appear in BMW jeeps, some confident, arrogant; others expressionless. Might there be any quiet dissenters – biding their time? Or is it just a job? Or have they gone to the dark side?

Those men (they are all men) are easy to hate. When their car has a baby seat I shout, 'your own kids are safe, you …' Our moderate chant, 'Shame on you!' doesn't sound strong enough.

I worry about my thoughts; a side of me wants to open the car door and tear this diplomat – spy – whatever he is – limb from limb, to do my bit for the resistance. I calm down when they drive away, even look at my phone and smile at another video of his countrymen being incinerated in a tank. A primitive, regrettable feeling. Better to imagine the peace of a blue and yellow horizon, clear skies, ripe wheat waving, as if beckoning a better tomorrow.

Summer Shells

John F (retired community worker, educator and researcher)

Fanore beach County Clare, my two grand-
     daughters at precious play,
Amid windy whirls and granular grains, the
     emerging castle holds all sway,
with nature's elegance, seashells, embellish
     their hand sanded display.

The kite overhead with its trailing tails I hold
     tight in the cloudless sky,
Summer sun on the glistening dunes, the
     waves lick-lap-leisurely and spy
on a scene so normal from a childhood tale to
     remain in my mind's eye.

In Ukraine, man-made shells from above
     shatter the innocents' peace
as calloused fingers on unsafety catches pre-
     pare for the deadly release
of shrapnel shards which scatter wide and
     ingrain deep in human flesh

children are maimed, disabled, and killed for
a demented despot's wish.

DOING SOMETHING

Deirdre (retired airline ground staff)

In the days leading up to the illegal invasion of Ukraine, the world was watching by satellite as the line-up of Russian military machinery reached the Ukraine border. Russia constantly denied their intention to invade in various interviews around the world. In an interview with the Russian ambassador to Ireland, he said, 'an invasion was a fantasy and the idea that Russia would invade Ukraine was insane'.

However, on Thursday 24 February 2022 the unthinkable happened and Russia invaded Ukraine. We watched on our televisions while innocent people, including the elderly, children and babies, were murdered by the Russians. Hospitals, schools and care homes and private homes were not exempt – mass murder was being committed everywhere. How could this be happening in 2022 and what constructive things could I do as an individual living in Ireland?

Initially, I made donations to various charities and went shopping for children's clothes to drop into the Ukrainian support shop in Clarendon Street but I still felt that I wasn't doing enough. My husband and I had joined weekend mass protests at the Russian embassy in the early days. While there I realised that this was something I could do, donate my time to protesting. Since then, I have been protesting there almost every week. Are we making a difference? We have all heard that quote 'The only thing necessary for the triumph of evil is for good men to do nothing' so as a good person I am doing something. We cannot ignore this illegal invasion by Russia on their sovereign neighbour Ukraine, otherwise we are complicit by default. That is exactly why I spend my time protesting.

While at the embassy you see the stark differences in lifestyles between the invaders and the invaded. The children in Ukraine are experiencing horrific atrocities that no child should ever endure, while we watch the children of the Russian embassy staff enjoying a great safe life in Dublin going to school, playing in the embassy grounds with no limitations on their meals. How can this be right? All Russian and Ukrainian children should be living safe and peaceful lives in their own sovereign countries. Neither should be victims of war!

It's over twelve months since the illegal invasion and my resolve and commitment are stronger than ever. The people of Ukraine have so impressed me – both the people I have met here in Dublin and the various interviews I have watched on television. They are very strong people and so committed to their country. Why wouldn't we in Ireland support them in whatever way we can? I am very grateful that in Ireland we live in a free society where our right to protest is protected. I understand that is not the case for many people around the world and in particular I am thinking of the good Russian people, who do not support the illegal invasion of Ukraine, but are forced to stay silent. I am protesting on their behalf as well.

I long for the day when I wake up to the news that the Russian troops are leaving Ukraine. We have a deep understanding of conflict on this island but we have enjoyed relatively peaceful times for almost twenty-five years. I hope that in the near future all Ukrainian people will be living free and peacefully like we are.

> Stop calling it war, for war implies faults on both sides. It's an invasion, where the state of Russia is the aggressor and the people of Ukraine are the victim.

ABHIJIT NASKAR (WORLD-FAMOUS SCIENTIST
AND ADVOCATE OF GLOBAL PEACE)

Reasons I Protest

Ann (pacifist and environmentalist)

I do it for my children and their children and
  the world they will inherit

I do it for the grandmothers left behind in
  shattered homes

I do it for the children blown apart

I do it for the women raped

I do it for the young men butchered

I do it for the Russians protesting

Is it useless?

Maybe

But to do nothing is worse
To do nothing makes me complicit.

Showing Solidarity

Brian C (retired social care worker)

I come to protest outside the Russian embassy to show my solidarity with the people of Ukraine and condemn unreservedly the Russian invasion and aggression against Ukraine and its population.

I wish to convey the cancellation of every single Céad Míle Fáilte ever offered to any member of the current Russian government and its agents. I also come to celebrate and honour the incredible freedom which we, as Irish citizens, enjoy.

Barbarians at the Gates of Lilliput

Brian P (who would rather be a frost person than a snowflake)

On 24 February 2022, in the third decade of the twenty-first century, having emerged groundhog-like from Covid isolation, the world discovered that Hitler had risen from his bunker and tanks were once again trundling westwards towards the European landscape. VlAdolf ratZputin (as I'll call him), a small shirtless man with big guns was on 'military manoeuvres' along the border with Ukraine. Yuri Filatov, the Russian ambassador to Ireland consoled fishermen and a 'hysterical' local population with repeated assurances that there was 'No intention to invade their neighbour'. With the first military jackboot on Ukrainian soil, the occupation had begun.

The Kremlin designated the ensuing brutal war a 'special military operation' to liberate Ukraine from the tyranny of fascism. An ill-disciplined horde emboldened by false premises and vodka was now engaging in atrocities perpetrated by the Nazis during the Second World War.

Russia and the West had persuaded Ukraine to relinquish its nuclear defence capability in exchange for the guarantee of territorial integrity. War now displaced women and children while fathers, sons and brothers remained to defend their homeland. Evidence of looting (washing machines!), rape and mass graves were refuted. Convicted criminals imprisoned by the Russian state for theft, rape and murder were conscripted to bolster a decimated Wagner group.[1]

The urban privileged and educated were exempt from the initial 'partial mobilisation' while hundreds of thousands outside Moscow who still reside under Stalin's shadow in a 1940s Soviet Union, and for whom socio-economic hardship is a patriotic duty, were summoned to a collapsing front. A desolate

---

1 *Russian paramilitary group – a mercenary army founded by the oligarch, Yevgeny Prigozhin.*

place commonly referred to as the Meat Grinder. Russians, like Ukrainian women and children before them, now flooded across neighbouring borders to escape the wrath of Putin's vanity and paranoia. To halt Ukraine's reclamation of her lands, sham referendums were hastily conducted to annex villages, towns and cities rendered uninhabitable by indiscriminate military destruction.

But what has any of this to do with standing on Orwell Road berating German cars which emerge from the gates of the Russian embassy? Behaviour perceived by some casual observers as incitement of passing traffic to provoke the use of car horns. The pastime of individuals who either need to 'get a life' or seek employment.

Realistically, the instigation of hostilities was outside the remit of the ambassador and his staff who are expected to endorse war in order to retain the privileges of Irish residency associated with deployment. Embassy business within the state had accountability imposed on 24 February and consequently 'diplomacy' could no longer be undertaken with the same impunity formerly taken for granted.

When an assumption that boredom would eventually become the architect of attrition, causing a departure of moral objectors and Ukrainian flags, did not materialise, inconvenience compounded embassy intransigence. The 'barbarians' at the gates were labelled 'frost people (otmoroski)' or thugs in the Russian media. Russophobes 'told to go and make a row,' despite cctv and photographic evidence that a less intimidating group would be difficult to assemble (*The Irish Times*, 16 August 2022). It is doubtful that any of their number would meet Wagner criteria and equally improbable that many embassy personnel will answer their presidential call to defend the motherland.

The West does not harbour an irrational contempt of Russia or her citizens, however civilised people cannot stand idly by when crimes against humanity are perpetrated. Proclaimed military manoeuvres were fraudulent. The 'special military operation' is a brutal war and illegal occupation of an independent, sovereign state. The Kremlin's deception of ordinary citizens will be exposed when enough Russian mothers ask why their husbands and sons are being dispatched to their deaths in a place, once welcoming, beyond Russia's vast borders.

Mutually Assured Destruction cannot be contained and the threat of an interminable global nuclear winter persists, but since the war began Ukraine has demonstrated great resolve and resilience. Our planet cannot accommodate another World War to appease or satiate the egos of Lilliputians in marble palaces who possess weapons of mass destruction. The narcissism of an autocrat in seclusion behind the Kremlin walls is 'unacceptable' to civilised nations and has brought global degradation to Russia's door.

Apathy is the opiate of authority. Never underestimate individual capacity to bring about change.

Remember the Ukrainian woman who

confronted Russian soldiers in her village, asking them 'why have you come here?' When no rational explanation was forthcoming she tried to persuade them to carry sunflower seeds in their pockets, so that in the event of their deaths, sunflowers would grow.

The protest at the Embassy of the Russian Federation, Orwell Road, Dublin (Photo: Declan Reid).

We accuse .... Ambassador Filatov arriving at the embassy (Photo: Declan Reid).

A Kremlin-style big brother keeps watch on Orwell Road
(Photo: Julian Vignoles).

Members of the protest group confront another embassy car
(Photo: Julian Vignoles).

Molly [bottom right] keeping a close eye on the protest
(Photo: John Farrelly).

Young Ukrainians in Ireland join the protest (Photo: Declan Reid).

Singing Ukraine's national anthem at Russia's embassy
(Photo: Declan Reid).

A moment of solidarity at the December 2022 vigil
(Photo: Ukrainian Action).

Orwell Road appropriately decorated
(Photo: Declan Reid).

Reading 'poetry against Putin' on day 200 of the invasion
(Photo: Declan Reid).

These colours don't run: afternoon sun illuminating Ukraine's flag (Photo: Tony Ryan).

We have often resorted to humour … (Photo: Declan Reid).

An alternative Russian voice at the embassy
(Photo: Declan Reid).

Contrasting colours on Orwell Road
(Photo: John Farrelly).

Presenting embassy staff with some realities of the war
(Photo: Declan Reid).

Banner designed by a member of the protesting group relays a truthful message (Photo: Declan Reid).

To a Russian General

Helen D (retired public servant)

What will you say when your grandchildren
Ask you what you did in the war?

Will you gaze into the distance and give
    them that silence,
To make sure they don't ask anymore?

Or will you tell them, 'I sent young men to
    hell,
I closed my eyes to atrocities,
I had no way out when I realised how far the
    war would go.
I offered my life to Russia and Russia took
    my soul.'

Reflections on the Protests

Colman (journalist)

Sometimes the ambassador's shiny Merc is sorely missed from the panto-like parade of BMWs when the Russian diplomats bolt for lunch. A chorus of 'Shame on you!', 'Náire!', 'Murderers!', 'Child killers!', 'Rapists!' and so forth awaits them at the gates. Contrast this with the nightly pictures of rusting tanks and abandoned hardware amid the pock-marked devastation as exhausted troops run back to Mother Russia to 'regroup', in the face of Ukrainian resistance.

The protest outside the embassy gates is an odd assembly, a sample of the politically aware for a particular age profile. It surfaced following the big-gun media splash in the early days that accompanied the presence of senior politicians as well as diplomats and trade union leaders on Orwell Road.

The ICTU led the jamboree that day across from the still-intact entrance. Ukraine's ambassador spoke feelingly, as did her counterparts from Poland, Lithuania and Georgia, each conscious of the other countries' susceptibilities amidst the rank odour of Putin on the march.

The day after the invasion Irish MEP Billy Kelleher's sign read: 'Ambassador Filatov, please go home. You are a Putin puppet and you have insulted the Irish people with your lies.'

And that, essentially, became the catch-cry as the ambassador sought to portray as reasonable the Kremlin's bombing of hospitals, the killing of children and whole families and the reduction of towns and cities to ashes. Less than a week earlier he was insisting it was ludicrous to suggest that Russian forces massing on Ukraine's border meant the Kremlin was poised to invade its neighbour. The Irish just didn't understand.

As media interest subsided, a definite chill developed towards Filatov and his staff. It grew into a determined rear-guard action.

The embassy's reaction to its entrance being vandalised by a reversing lorry, along with the red-painted swastikas on the walls, was one of seething indignation. Less than diplomatic notes were hurled at the Department of Foreign Affairs and the Garda Síochána on a daily basis. Garda patrols were employed outside the embassy to ensure the peace was kept, courtesy of the Irish taxpayer. In effect, it meant a garda had to lift the barricade each time a Russian motorcade, or even a single vehicle, emerged from or entered the embassy grounds.

This ludicrous situation sparked a burst of creativity among a hard-core of some thirty to fifty male and female protesters. One woman, say Hash Tag 14, undertook the sewing of Ukrainian coloured (blue and yellow) ribbons onto the hedge opposite the embassy – and they have remained there, virtually pristine, for more than twelve months. Hash Tag 13 emerged with a plethora of posters that leave little to the imagination as regards Russian atrocities and disdain for human rights.

Similarly, Hash Tags 25, 18, 31, 20 and 12 came up with particularly apposite depictions of Putin and the imperial Russian mindset. One in particular captures, appropriately, the Kremlin's misinterpretation of history: in its failure to evolve its legitimacy from Peter the Great (a Europhile, ironically, in his love of the industrial revolution), to the less than great Vladimir Putin.

And then came Hash Tag 23, a distinguished tenor, who taught the group to sing the Ukrainian national anthem, with mixed results. No matter, it maddened the Russians inside the embassy, and perhaps explains the continuing increase in furtive iPhone clicking each day from inside the 'Beamers' as the gates fly open (courtesy of a new electronic system) for the hungry diplomats.

Why I Protest

Denis (retired laboratory manager)

Like everyone I was outraged by the Russian invasion of Ukraine and I wondered what I, as an ordinary citizen, could do about it. As I live within walking distance of the Russian embassy I decided that this presented an opportunity to register my abhorrence at this out-rage in a practical way. So, I took myself up there and was greatly encouraged to find that I was not alone. Instead, I found like-minded Irish citizens, though all strangers to me, doing exactly the same thing. That is making it clear to the ambassador and his staff there, who come and go quite regularly, our disgust and horror at what Vladimir Putin has unleashed on the Ukrainian people.

One of my initial reactions to the invasion, I am ashamed to admit, was disappointment that the visit of the St Petersburg Ballet to Dublin in March 2022 was cancelled. I had booked to go with two of my daughters. However, I was given a reality check quite quickly when I spoke with the Ukrainian manager of my local coffee shop. I go there for coffee and a scone after my weekly swim. While his mother and sister-in-law had safely arrived in Ireland, though the latter's husband remained on duty with the Ukrainian army, his own mother and sister were stuck in Kyiv which was at that time under bombardment and threat from Russian troops. They finally escaped to Poland but have since returned to Ukraine as his nephew was due to start school in September 2022.

In the meantime, I have bought a Ukrainian flag which I bring along with me whenever I am 'on duty'. I tend to go up to the embassy in the morning when the public office is open. There is usually a steady stream of people, Russian I presume, sorting out their paperwork or other documents or visas. It is as much for their benefit as that of the staff, who are probably indifferent to my presence, that I am protesting.

Not that I have any enmity for them, the

average Russian citizen, they are as oppressed, in a different way, as the Ukrainians. However, it is as important to make clear to them the outrage felt by the Irish people at the actions of Vladimir Putin. Their only other source of information, in Russia, is state controlled media and propaganda. At least they can communicate the protest at their embassy to their friends and relations back home and make them aware, like the friends and relatives of the ballet company, how the free world has reacted to the invasion of Ukraine.

A Story of Why and Who Knows

Des (retired business executive)

'Why?' crops up a lot in the context of Ukraine. Answers to it rather less often. I have made my own attempt, but opinions are easy and only have as much value as you put on them.

Why did Russia invade Ukraine? Because it could. It satisfies a yearning for a return to an extended Russian empire. Indeed, it is not just in Ukraine that Russia has been trying to add to its territory but also by interference in Georgia and Moldova. And it is not just Putin, much though we would like to believe that.

Why do civilians have to die? Because wars are no longer fought only by soldiers but are waged on populations. Russia cynically denies this as it tries to bring the civilian population to its knees. It is easier than defeating an army they think.

Why does Russia not just crush Ukraine with its military might, including nuclear options? Because it under-estimated the Ukrainian will to resist to answer the first part. Fear of NATO for the second part, much though some may not like that thought.

Why do we protest? Each has their own reasons. Me, because I hate the inhumanity of what Russia is doing and the suffering it is causing; I want to say that to Russians, who are actively involved in propaganda about their 'special operation'. I am angry when I hear their lies and need to express that anger. Why are more people not protesting? Who knows? Too busy with their own lives? Can't be bothered? Don't feel anything for the Ukrainians? Don't think their voices would make any difference? Most likely it is just in-difference.

Why is it mainly older people in the protest? Who knows? If the USA had invaded a country and was shelling, bombing and killing innocent civilians daily I think there would be thousands of young people outside the US embassy chanting their opposition.

So where are the students and the trade unions and the political parties? Who knows?

Occasional politicians are not wholly unknown, though for photograph opportunities or to criticise NATO mainly. It seems that left leaning parties do not like to criticise the left, though Putin is hardly left – merely an evil autocrat – but he escapes strong criticism from such politicians I think because it is Russia, not the West. But it's not about left and right, but suffering and pain, life and death, right and wrong and, yes, good and evil.

Why bother then? Because someone has to hold Russia to account. Someone has to say your lies are just that. Someone has to say that people dying because of your invasion is immoral. Someone has to say that the terrible deeds of your soldiers are war crimes. Someone has to say that destroying innocent people's lives is heart-breaking. Someone has to say this is all wrong. Someone has to stand up, stand outside and say 'shame on you' – again and again.

We are a few older people, well behaved and make little noise, but if a lot of people made a little noise more people might hear our messages. Who knows? Why? Because the alternative is to give up, do nothing and not show we care. The Russians would like that.

Time to Stand

Eibhlín (mother of seven and Mamo to nine, genealogist)

Time must be made, I stand in protest
Don't tell me about other places
It's not colour or creed that got me
This one reached out to me
Domination by a powerful neighbour!!!!!!
No respect for democracy – a people already
free

Putin's army and its trail of destruction
City after city bombarded and levelled
Schools, hospitals, every bit of infrastructure
Living spaces all levelled, pummelled into the
ground
Not a remnant to be rescued from the rubble
Memories are all that are left to those who
have survived

There are commonalities with Ireland's past
Centuries of colonisation and domination
Before my time, but not really – I research,

I delve into the archives, bridging the gaps
The destitute Irish fleeing our shores, the
coffin ships
People without hope, dependent on the good
will of others
I do my bit with their descendants, filling in
the gaps
My family survived and prospered here.

Now I have a voice, freedom to protest
Here I stand, I have no fear, no one to protect
I can smile when I see 'intimidation' in action
Behaviours unbecoming, belittle the person
who seeks to provoke
It raises a smile – one small victory for me
I see humanity, the odd time, it matters but
I am only responsible for myself and my
actions
I still stand and have no fear.

Vacancies for People with a Conscience

Eugene (former army officer, airline captain and aviation consultant)

Having spent many years working in a variety of African countries, I found the tribal issues were never very far below the surface. These issues were not helped by colonial powers drawing straight lines on the map of Africa outlining different countries. These 'borders' frequently divided traditional territories and at the very least, left a legacy of discontent, if not open warfare. Genocide came to Rwanda in 1994, when the ruling Hutu tribe, via their armed militias, attempted to exterminate their minority compatriots, the Tutsi tribe, causing the deaths of approximately one million people. Europe then felt a long way away.

It did then come as quite a shock, to find that in 2022, Russia had reverted to its Soviet Union/colonial past and began its 'special military operation'/illegal invasion of Ukraine. This shock was partly due to the seeming paralysis that overcame world organisations that we normally rely on for security; the UN, NATO, the United States, and the European Defence Agency. It seemed that Russia could take what it wished in the first ten days of the war, while the West got to grips with this new reality. This now involves hundreds, if not thousands of investigations into alleged war crimes, genocide, targeting of civilian areas and crimes of rape. We await the results of these investigations.

Having been an army officer in my youth, I do feel slightly impotent regarding the level of my contribution to the defence of freedoms in Ukraine. However, impending old age and creaky joints would render me more of a liability than an asset. I find that protesting is the food for one's conscience, and just like our daily food diet, needs regular refuelling. I have been very lucky to meet some wonderful citizens of obvious high integrity on our protest outside the Russian embassy. Our numbers have been small, generally six to ten people at any one time, but our ambition to achieve justice for the people of Ukraine is sky high. Ireland has always punched well above its weight on the world stage, and I would appeal to any citizen reading this, that if you feel strongly about this illegal war and you have time available, come and join us.

From M.A.D. to M.A.C.A.

Lorraine (visual artist)

My first real understanding of the Ukrainian invasion came when my next-door neighbour had her son's mother-in-law join her household. Although she had no English, this lady was delighted when I brought her a 'Welcome to Ireland' written on a chocolate cake. Her stress and worry over family left in Ukraine was deep-felt and harrowing for her.

Then I heard an eloquent interview with John Farrelly on radio and I was hooked by his clarity, one word in particular stuck – for Russia to 'withdraw'. That got me. You hear about evil happening when we don't stand up – in Ireland we have the right to protest – we should use it, so I joined the continuous protest outside the Russian embassy.

I don't wish to conflate the war in Ukraine with a similar awakening I had while studying at NCAD (National College of Art and

Design). I was researching an essay on 'Art/ Place and Human Geography' and read that about forty thousand people were being displaced because their towns and villages were built over lignite coal in the Düsseldorf/ Cologne region named Garzweiler. So many people's lives, their homes, schools, hospitals, farms, businesses were all displaced to access this lignite coal. This brown coal is classified as the lowest rank of coal, of which only twenty-five per cent is used, meaning seventy-five per cent is parked, creating mountains the size of Benbulben.

This brought me on a five-to-six-year work plan which included the topic of climate change. And as the school kids doing street protests holding banners put it 'THERE IS NO PLANET B'.

We need to listen. If we could listen to Greta Thunberg and Mohamed Bouazizi, a twenty-six-year-old street vendor in Tunisia who self-immolated in protest of his treatment by local officials, whose subsequent death led to the Arab Spring uprising.

Let's look too at the 'Occupy' movement which, inspired by the Arab Spring, took action over US government corruption and then ten years later the racial injustice protests of 2020 after the killing of George Floyd. The Occupy movement spread to nine hundred cities worldwide and showed what is possible when a haphazard group of protesters turn private suffering into public action.

These issues can collectively highlight our road to M.A.D. 'Mutual Assured Destruction'. Instead, let's defy Vladimir Putin's use of fossil fuels as ammunition, and instead combine our own powers by converting to renewables. Let's call this M.A.C.A. 'Mutually Assured Climate Action' – to stop wars and save our planet for the next generation(s).

Right to Dissent and Duty to Protest

Helen F (coffee and chocolate aficionado)

During the past few years, I have frequently thought about how fortunate we are living in a country where we can, within legal limits, express our opinions openly. I can vote in meaningful local and national elections, in genuine referendums, and I can join a political party, either mainstream or opposition. When I meet politicians face to face, I can tell them what I think of their actions, I can lobby, ask for progress reports or for assistance. When all these fail, I could express my views or opposition, either by writing letters, marching, usually down O'Connell Street, or standing outside Dáil Éireann. When I do this, I am protected by the gardaí and the state.

In many other countries, I cannot openly express any opinions contrary to the regime or diktats of the ruler. If I did, I could be threatened with assault by police. I could face imprisonment or even death for the same reasons. However, in this country I have a right, to openly dissent. When does this right to protest become a duty? I am unsure. If I wish to support those who cannot openly express dissent, is there an obligation to protest on their behalf? Over the years I have stood on Kildare Street, outside many embassies and walked in groups, large and small through the streets of Dublin. Usually, it's on behalf of people who cannot safely do this and I am a token voice. I am fulfilling a duty.

I occasionally stand outside the embassy of Russia to protest the invasion of Ukraine. Not only are the people of Ukraine coping with death, injury, terror, hunger, loss of homes, farms and futures but alongside them, the plain people of Russia, the families of the soldiers tricked and forced into an unjust war suffer with them. In both countries, their future and their children's future are being ruined and I must protest.

ODE TO YURI FILATOV

Mark (retired UK government public servant)

Yuri Filatov Ambassador extraordinaire
He of the thin moustache and jet black hair

He's Putin's lackey on this misty green isle
A role he relishes behind a crocodile smile

He cruises about in his big black merc
With an insincere grin and an oily smirk

He bestrides the airwaves on behalf of Vlad
'Invade Ukraine? You must be mad!'
'

He's got the talk show hosts under his thumb
'Russia aggressive? Do you think I am dumb!'

But what Yuri misses when he reports back
after
Is that everyone he meets convulses with
laughter.

What Could I Do?

Jean (retired library assistant, mother and grandmother)

I was shocked to hear on 24 February 2022 that Russian troops had crossed the border into the sovereign territory of Ukraine. When Russian military manoeuvres were taking place nearby, I never believed it would come to this, even though both the EU and Ukraine were worried. We were assured by Vladimir Putin and Russian ambassador to Ireland, Yuri Filatov that they had no intention of doing this. It seems even the Russian troops themselves did not know.

How could this be happening in a country that had hosted the Eurovision Song Contest just a few years previously in which both Russia and Ireland had participated? In fact, Ukraine was to host it again in 2022. How could both countries have taken part in different sporting events over the last few years and now be at war? How could one of those countries invade another and what could be achieved but suffering, destruction and also huge displacement of the population, creating a refugee problem for them and requiring major support from the EU and ourselves?

What could I do, just one person? I went to some early demonstrations and a big protest march from the Ukrainian embassy to the Russian embassy with some like-minded friends. But this wasn't enough, and the war continued. So, I started to go most weeks to protest outside the embassy. The people who were there became familiar faces that I recognised each time I came. I was very impressed by their dedication and commitment. I began to feel part of a 'tribe'. I could see that we were having some effect. It seems that we were labelled the Russian equivalent of 'thugs' in an interview with Ambassador Filatov on Russian television. I hope I was included in that.

So, I'm not just one person but part of a small group that make themselves seen and heard and won't be ignored.

I am also amazed at the bravery of the Ukrainian people and especially President Zelenskyy. But sad when I hear of the killings and destruction wrought on Ukraine and its people. I pray that a solution will soon be found that will bring an end to this madness.

Slava Ukraini!

PROTESTING ON ORWELL ROAD

John D (retired police officer)

I'm not quite sure how I came to be part of the protest group outside the Russian embassy. I can remember the first time I went there – it was in late February 2022, after the invasion had begun and a big protest was taking place, presumably organised by the Ukrainian community who are living in Ireland. The numbers attending were impressive and I bumped into quite a few people I knew. In the days following there was a lot of media coverage of the invasion and the horrors it was visiting upon the people of Ukraine. There were lots of appeals for aid and I made my donation to the Red Cross hoping it would go towards helping somebody somewhere in Ukraine.

Then I sat back and settled into my normal life pattern. Part of that pattern was to keep up with the daily news, which at that time consisted in large part of reports on events in Ukraine. Each and every night harrowing scenes were displayed on the television screen with particular emphasis on the mass exodus of refugees from the country. People forced to flee from their homes and families and as the song says packing all of their hopes in a matchbox. Women and children desperately trying to board trains heading anywhere so long as the direction was west. Elderly people, too frail, too tired, too long in the tooth, choosing to stay put and hope against hope.

I asked a friend of mine if he would stay and head to the front line if he had been born in Ukraine and was very impressed when he replied without hesitation that you would have to. I said I'd do the same and imagined myself and Tony holding back the Russian army for all of two, maybe three seconds. Laughable really. But it occurred to me that that was exactly what was in store for thousands of young and not so young men from across the cities and towns of Ukraine. People enlisting as opposed to being drafted. From within

Ukraine's borders and much further afield. And that set me thinking.

Following the latest news of the invasion from the safety of my living room chair was not good enough anymore. The question was, what could I do? Living in Dublin, so far removed from what was going on, the answer was nothing really. Making another donation to the Red Cross didn't ease my conscience for very long. For whatever reason, and I don't know why, I decided to go back down to Orwell Road. I even made an A4 sized poster and wrote 'Putin Murderer' on it. I realised just how crappy my poster was when I got to Orwell Road and saw what others had. But what impressed me even more was that there were people there at all, some of whom had been protesting for weeks at that point. I was made to feel welcome and quickly began to feel at home with the protesters. So, at home over twelve months later I still feel the need to regularly turn up to embarrass and discomfort the Russian diplomats and spies as they enter and exit the embassy. I am not so sure that any of those working in the embassy can be embarrassed or made to feel any discomfort. They seem pretty impervious to it all, water off a duck's back as it were. I know for certain that it makes no difference at all to the war in Ukraine. I have heard that Ukrainians living in Ireland are appreciative of our efforts and I hope that is true.

But sometimes I do wonder what, if anything, the protest is achieving? The protest group could quite easily be described as simply a loose collection of individuals with no stated aims or organised hierarchy. What it does have is a fierce determination 'to see this through to the end'. What that means depends on each individual member. For me the end comes when the Russian army leaves Ukrainian soil. How long before that might happen I don't know. In the meantime, I will continue to call for Russian war criminals to get out of Ukraine. Loudly.

Shared Steps in Protest

Jack H (retired public servant)

We gather outside the Russian Embassy on
    Dublin's Orwell Road,
To show the Ukrainian people that we're
    symbolically helping to carry their load,
To demonstrate our disbelief, sadness, anger
    and absolute rage,
At the unjustified war the Russian regime on
    their neighbour wage,

We carry banners, messages and slogans,
    wrapped in blue and gold,
Cloths stitched together and flags of GAA
    counties, a joy to behold,
Passing cars slow down and honk their horns,
    bikes ring their bell,
Human togetherness creating a huge sup-
    portive groundswell.

As the days pass, protest fatigue and the
    routines of life see our numbers dwindle,

And we wonder how on earth the initial
    momentum we can rekindle,
At embassy cars entering and leaving the
    compound we vent our ire,
The energy it gives lifts our spirits, ensures
    our vigil will not expire.

Standing with Ukraine, despite the rain
(Photo: Declan Reid).

Summer in Dublin solidarity
(Photo: Alan Betson/*Irish Times*).

A lone protester keeps vigil
(Photo: Declan Reid).

Ambassador Filatov getting a taste of the protest – again
(Photo: Alan Betson/*Irish Times*).

Seasons come and go, solidarity with Ukraine goes on
(Photo: Declan Reid).

Doing time on the picket line, summer 2022
(Alan Betson/*Irish Times*).

A protestor at the embassy entrance
(Photo: Declan Reid).

Image of an innocent victim on a pillar at the embassy entrance (Photo: Declan Reid).

An evening vigil at the embassy
(Photo: Declan Reid).

Alternative Russian crests at the embassy gates
(Photo: Declan Reid).

Protesters awaiting the return of the ambassador and his staff
(Photo: Declan Reid).

Protest ongoing
(Photo: Julian Vignoles).

The Grim Reaper's message for Putin
(Photo: Declan Reid).

Wave Bye-Bye – We're Off to Mars!

Lorraine (visual artist)

Before we go, let's look at the world we're leaving behind. This Post Modern age of undermining truth, facts, accountability, reality, responsibility, justice, caring for the 'other' person – in essence turning humanity on its head and burying it in the ground in full view and in plain sight. Given this Post Modern time where Vladimir Putin can send troops into the Donbas region under the guise of 'peacekeepers' to stop the alleged carnage being perpetrated by Ukraine on separatists in the region. These lies were just the beginning.

What if this unjust war continues for more than a few years? Can we envisage having both Vladimir Putin and possibly Donald Trump at war? Will we have the Third World War by then? Will we be wiped out by a meteor, or face extinction by the climate change we are too busy to deal with? Or maybe we'll be squeezed together onto one continent due to climate change and learn how to accommodate each other. Could we do that?

I'd like to think and hope we can grow sense and actually appreciate what we have here on earth. If I could take up some of your time to read this extract from William Shatner's book *Boldly Go: Reflections on a Life of Awe and Wonder.* The *Star Trek* actor who played Captain Kirk on the starship *Enterprise*, reflects on his voyage into space on Jeff Bezos' 'Blue Origin' space shuttle in October 2021. Shatner at ninety years of age became the oldest living person to travel into space, but he was surprised by his own reaction to the experience:

> I saw a cold, dark, black emptiness. It was unlike any blackness you can see or feel on earth. It was deep, enveloping, all-encompassing. I turned back toward the light of home ...
>
> The contrast between the vicious coldness of space and the warm nurturing of earth below filled me with overwhelming sadness. Every day we are confronted with the knowledge of further

destruction of earth at our own hands... things that took five billion years to evolve and suddenly we will never see them again because of the interference of mankind ...

My trip to space was supposed to be a celebration; instead, it felt like a funeral.

In short we now live on a planet made up of humans who need to make their search for truth and authenticity heard and respected. We need to have an informed media that works towards global political co-operation and international fairness for human rights, a media committed to the development of critical thinking skills to expose lies and corruption. This is not only about Russia; it also includes weaknesses relating to the political realm of Western powers which impact on the effectiveness of democracy. Our world has become more complex, resulting in sometimes unintended consequences based on trumped up fear and hatred.

I'll leave you with the thoughts of another author, Frank White, writing on the shift of cognitive awareness when viewing our planet from outer space and experiencing the earth with an increased sense of connection to other people, plus the earth as a whole, from his book *The Overview Effect* in 1987:

> There are no borders or boundaries on our planet except those that we create in our minds or through human behaviours. All the ideas and concepts that divide us when we are on the surface begin to fade from orbit and the moon. The result is a shift in worldview and in identity. It can change the way we look at the planet but also other things like countries, ethnicities, religions; it can prompt an instant re-evaluation of our shared harmony and a shift in focus to all the wonderful things we have in common instead of what makes us different … that allows us perhaps a chance to rededicate ourselves to our planet, to each other, to life and love all around us. If we seize that chance.

Shhh! Don't tell anyone, only some of us will go to Mars.

Nite, nite, sleep well.

To a Young Russian Conscript

Helen D (retired public servant)

Fifty years from now when you sit alone
By the fireside in your little home
In rural Russia
You will look deep into the flames
And you will see the faces of the children
Of Ukraine.

You will see the apartment blocks you bombed
The shopping malls reduced to rubble
The maternity hospitals levelled
By your shells.

And when the fire dies down
And there is nothing left but embers
You will climb the dark stairs
To your narrow bed
And you will tell yourself,
'I fought for my country,

I followed orders –
I was not human then.'

Beware Russians Driving Tanks

Maureen (retired bank official)

In 1956 as a young eight-year-old I was getting ready to go to school listening to the nine o'clock news on Raidió Éireann. As my mother brushed my hair, I heard the newscaster say that Russian tanks had entered the Hungarian capital of Budapest to quell the uprising. Many civilians were losing their lives. It was very frightening to my young ears even without graphic images or analysis from military experts or indeed on-the-spot reporting. I knew little of Hungary and my only knowledge of Russia was that in church we were praying for its conversion. But something was not right.

It might be worth mentioning at this stage that in 1950s Ireland the only contact with the outside world was from the wireless and newspapers. Raidió Éireann transmitted for about ten hours per day. BBC Radio was available but certainly not the twenty-four-hour coverage we have today. Ireland had no television station – that only happened on 31 December 1961, and few were able to afford a television set which could pick up the BBC.

Fast forward to 1961, more Russian tanks entered East Berlin to help with the erection of the now infamous Wall and ensure that East Germany would now operate under the watchful eye of the USSR behind the Iron Curtain. In 1968 their tanks again entered the city of Prague making sure that the then Czechoslovakia would remain shackled to their ideology.

Many decades later that eight-year-old girl, now a retired adult, was deeply shocked to listen to the news again on 24 February 2022 and hear that Russian tanks once more were on the move this time to illegally invade a sovereign independent Ukraine. A country with a population of forty plus million, which had set out on the path to democracy on 24 August 1991, internationally recognised, a member of the United Nations and as stated in Article 1 of their written constitution: 'Ukraine is a sovereign and independent, democratic, social and law based State.'

I had to do something, but what? I can support humanitarian aid. President Zelenskyy said in one of his inspiring speeches if you can do nothing else but protest, do so. I also thought of my maternal grandmother who as an eighteen-year-old took part in the 1916 Irish Rising for Independence. Is there something in the Irish psyche that makes it difficult for us to witness injustice? As a race we dislike masters. John Boyle O'Reilly (1844–1890) an Irish Fenian, patriot, poet and editor describes it well in 'Erin':

> May no weak race be wronged, and no strong robber feared
>
> To oppressors more hateful, to slaves more endeared,
> Till the World comes to know that the test of a cause
>
> Is the hatred of tyrants and Erin's applause.

That is why I now come to the Russian embassy to regularly remind the ambassador and his diplomatic staff that as long as his country's invading forces continue with their unprovoked war on Ukraine the good people of that state will continue to have my 'applause'.

Slava Ukraini!

STANDING WITH UKRAINE

Patrick (former public servant)

Following on the evil of the Russian invasion of Ukraine on 24 February 2022 and despite my individual sense of helplessness, John Stuart Mill's aphorism about the triumph of evil was the main driving force behind my personal ongoing protest outside the Russian embassy. Quite clearly good men and women – and especially western democracies – did not do enough to counter the Russian invasion of Georgia in 2008, nor the Russian annexation of Crimea in 2014 – with not a single shot being fired – or indeed the subsequent Russian armed support for separatists in eastern Donbas. Appeasement on these previous occasions led Russia to think that the much greater and bolder adventure of invading and annexing all of Ukraine was well within their grasp. And if this succeeded, why should they stop there?

As the Russian tanks rolled into northern Ukraine at dawn on 24 February, I reminded myself of the treachery and duplicity of Mr Putin and his acolytes who in the weeks and months before the invasion, despite massing over one hundred thousand troops and their weapons of war on the Russian/Ukrainian border, were continuously assuring Ukraine and the wider world that they had no intention whatever of invading. Then there was the arrogance of the Russian president in the days before the invasion when he asserted that Russia and Ukraine were one nation and furthermore that Ukraine did not have a right to exist as a separate state. I reflected on the blatantly false statement made by the representative of the Russian government in Ireland, Ambassador Filatov, when, on 2 February – just three weeks before the invasion – he appeared before the Oireachtas Joint Committee on Foreign Affairs and Defence. In his written submission to the Committee, he stated:

> We are witnessing the daily drumbeat about [the] 'imminent Russian invasion in Ukraine' as well

as [the] readiness by the West to respond to that 'invasion' with massive and destructive sanctions against Russia. Any unbiased and serious observer would note, that not only are there no facts on the ground to support such [an] 'invasion' fantasy, not only Russia has stated repeatedly that it does not have any intention to attack Ukraine or anybody else, but there are not even hypothetically any political, economic, military or any other reasons for such [an] invasion.

As we now know, the false and perfidious nature of these assurances was exposed when Russian tanks invaded Ukraine at dawn on 24 February along with bombardment by land, sea and air of both military and civilian facilities with consequent devastating loss of life. The appalling brutality gratuitously visited on a fledgling democracy by a much larger and powerful autocracy driven by its own imperial ambitions seemed to be taking Europe right back to the early twentieth and even the nineteenth century.

In the interest of respecting every country's national sovereignty and future international peace and security, it was vital that democratic countries responded in the way they did by imposing extensive sanctions on Russia and providing financial, humanitarian and military support to Ukraine in repelling Russian aggression. I am particularly proud of the speedy support provided to Ukraine by the EU and its member states and especially the warm welcome and support afforded by Ireland to the refugees fleeing the war in Ukraine.

Furthermore, at an individual level, I feel there is an onus on us to show our abhorrence at the blatant injustice and immorality of Russia's actions in Ukraine and the resultant suffering, slaughter and destruction that it has imposed on the people of Ukraine. As we learn about atrocity after atrocity, the evil nature of Russia's invasion is being fully revealed.

This is why I have been standing for Ukraine outside the Russian embassy since the war began on 24 February 2022 and why I continue to do so until an outcome satisfactory to the people and government of Ukraine is achieved.

First Time Protesters

Rose Marie (chemist and retired director)

24 February 2022, Dublin; shock and horror at Russia's illegal invasion of Ukraine.

We woke from Covid hibernation to the realisation that what we thought was consigned to history books, was now happening in our lifetime. Maybe our own history, with our near neighbour, made us feel it more acutely?

Watching events unfold in the media, with the immediacy of twenty-first century communications, we felt helpless, hopeless and stirred to act and bear witness against the atrocities of war, at the Russian embassy – first time protesters.

What If?

Valerie (mother and pacifist)

As your military continues to bombard Ukrainian cities, deliberately targeting innocent civilians, in an unprovoked attack, Russia, take a minute to consider, what if it were me or my family?

Consider the sick and the elderly, dragged from their homes on makeshift stretchers and trollies. Terrified, traumatised and in pain, their homes destroyed and a lifetime of memories obliterated in an instant, now facing an uncertain future somewhere far from their homes.

Consider the old woman, brutalised and terrorised, her husband dragged away by your soldiers for no reason other than the fact he was Ukrainian. Her days spent searching the streets and bombed out buildings and basements, to finally find his body and having to dig a grave for him with her bare hands. Ask yourself, what if they were my grandparents?

Consider the child, beaten, raped and forced to watch the murder of her parents and her dog. Physically and emotionally damaged for the rest of her life. Ask yourself, what if she was my little girl?

Consider the father, sitting for hours in the street beside the body of his murdered twelve-year-old son, torn between leaving his son's body and searching for his thirteen-year-old daughter, critically injured by the shelling of their home. Ask yourself, what if this man was my father?

Consider the patients in the hospitals as they come under attack from your shells. Terrified pregnant women and delicate new-born babies forced to take shelter in basements as doctors and nurses try to keep them alive while risking their own lives. Ask yourself, what if this was your wife and new-born child?

Russia, stop this savage, senseless and un-provoked attack and leave Ukraine in peace.

Consider the dead, the maimed and the millions of displaced people who, while grateful for the sanctuary offered by other countries, simply want to go home.

Ask yourself, what if it were me?

Glóir don Úcráin, Glóir do na Laochra

Críostóir (retired and proud Dublin football supporter)

I am a child of the 1960s, and events from that era stick out in my memory – and have influenced me to this day – like the shooting of J.F. Kennedy and Martin Luther King, Vietnam and the anti-war movement, the growth of the civil rights movement in America and the emergence of the civil rights movement in Northern Ireland.

I have a particular memory of the infamous People's Democracy 'Long March' from Belfast to Derry in 1969, and I can still recall my anger at seeing the black and white television images of civil rights protesters being attacked during that march on Burntollet Bridge.

'Free Derry' became the 'town I loved so well' and I followed news from there with great interest. The events of Bloody Sunday outraged me to a point where I joined the thousands who stood outside the British embassy on Merrion Square on that fateful day in 1972 when it was burned down. I was an innocent, naïve, idealistic thirteen-year-old then who felt he had to do something, to protest and to demonstrate his anger at the killing of innocent people fighting for their civil rights.

So began my 'induction' to protesting and my on-going interest in civil rights both at home and abroad. In particular, I followed the extraordinary and sometimes tragic events and changes that took place in Poland, East Germany, Romania, Bulgaria, Albania and Czechoslovakia throughout the 1980s/early 1990s with great interest. I've protested against Reagan's visit to Ireland, marched against the Gulf War, indeed I've probably protested outside more embassies over the years than I'd care to remember.

Like most people, I first began to develop an interest in Ukraine around the time of the Chernobyl disaster and its horrible aftermath. My interest in Ukraine increased with the huge protests that took place in 2004 when Ukrainians took to the streets in what became known as The Orange Revolution. These protests were in response to claims that the presidential election had been rigged in favour of the pro-Russian candidate, Yanukovych. An assassination attempt by poisoning had been made on the opposition candidate Victor Yushchenko during that election, which he survived, having been flown to and treated in a hospital in Austria. Ukraine's Supreme Court finally broke the political deadlock. The court decided that due to the scale of the electoral fraud it became impossible to establish the election results. Therefore, it invalidated the official results that would have given Yanukovych the presidency, the protests ended, a second round of voting took place with Yushchenko winning fifty-two per cent of the votes that time round to Yanukovych's forty-four per cent. People power ultimately won the day.

In 2013, Ukrainians were once again forced to take to the streets, this time to protest at their government's (now led by Yanukovych) sudden decision not to sign the 'European Union–Ukraine Association Agreement', instead choosing closer ties to Russia and the Eurasian Economic Union. And this even though Ukraine's parliament had over-whelmingly approved finalising the agreement with the EU, but Russia had put pressure on Ukraine to reject it. Over half a million Ukrainians took part in this peaceful uprising known as Euromaidan/ Revolution of Dignity. These protests started in November and continued through until February 2014 when, following clashes with Berkut special riot police, over one hundred protesters and thirteen police officers were killed. Soon after Yanukovych fled to Russia. The accusations from Moscow that the protesters killed were all armed, brought memories of Bloody Sunday to mind.

The rest is history and, despite efforts and attempts by Ukraine to move further away from Russian influence, Ukrainians today find themselves not only fighting for their civil rights, but also fighting against an invasion by their bigger and more powerful 'neighbour'; fighting for their homes; fighting for their lives and, ultimately, fighting for their right to exist as an independent and sovereign state.

I am no longer an innocent, naïve thirteen-year-old, but I haven't yet lost my idealism. In a sense it is impossible for me to 'stand idly by' and to watch an invasion of a country whose struggle I have followed for nearly twenty years, as it continually attempts to break the yoke of Russian control and domination.

And that is why I choose to stand outside the Russian embassy, it is my tiny personal protest against Putin/Russia's invasion of Ukraine, and my way of demonstrating my support for Ukraine and its people.

> Our lives begin to end the day we become silent about things that matter.
>
> (Martin Luther King Jr)

WE'RE ALL UKRAINIANS NOW

Paul (retired, active and engaged)

Growing up in the 1970s, I remember watching *The World at War* documentary series. It made a profound impression on me, especially the sight of bewildered families dragging suitcases along bombed-out streets as they sought refuge from terrible conflict during the 1939–45 period.

So, when heart-breaking images of civilians in Ukraine suffering the same type of displacement, death and destruction reached our screens in spring 2022, my reaction was a mixture of outrage and anger against the Russian Federation for its illegal invasion, and sympathy for Ukrainian people subjected to such barbarity.

I think the daily gathering of protesters outside the embassy of the Russian Federation in Ireland achieves three things. It tells the

Russian delegation that Irish citizens are implacably opposed to their regime's brutal war, which contravenes international law and insults human decency. It lets our Ukrainian friends know that their trauma is in our hearts and will never be forgotten. And it keeps the cause of Ukraine alive in the eyes and ears of cyclists, motorists and pedestrians who pass the embassy each day.

Because the threat to Ukraine is existential, every aspect of Ukrainian national life and culture plays a part in highlighting this grave injustice. The power of music to move and motivate is widely understood, and I can think of no greater expression of solidarity than to sing Ukraine's national anthem outside the gates of the Russian embassy. Having learned the melody and lyrics, I am proud and honoured that fellow protesters join with me in making a musical statement that says:

> Ukraine Exists. Ukraine Endures. Ukraine Will Not Be Subjugated.

The title of the anthem, *Shche ne vmerla*

Ukrayiny, translates as 'Ukraine has not yet perished'. Written as a patriotic poem by Pavlo Chubynsky, an ethnographer, in 1862, it was set to music the following year by Mykhailo Verbytsky, a Ukrainian composer and Greek Catholic priest.

One hundred and sixty years later, the anthem's defiance and expression of hope for a better future captures the mood of the daily protest on Orwell Road.

We're all Ukrainians now.

A Grave Message

John F (retired community worker, educator and researcher)

I once was a parent living in Izyum but sadly
    no longer am,
My precious children I dearly loved they
    nestled in my arms,
I relished the spring and autumn too the
    shimmering stars at night,
till war exploded through my door and
    extinguished my life light.

Smithereened Delph upon my floors bear the
    print of the occupiers' hand,
Smashed television screen and broken chairs
    signal his hateful band,
The rugs and throws in my living room no
    need for all them now,
For I exist in another world where ghostly
    spectres reign and row.

Callously dumped in a sandy grave marked
    with a crude cross,

Amongst pine trees with many others who
 suffered similar loss,
Brutally tortured, slaughtered and denied all
 dignity and grace,
A nameless numbered nondescript pit my
 final resting place.

No longer a purely physical form just a
 shadowy former self,
I miss the china that adorned my table and
 the kitchen shelves,
No soft music soothes the angry wounds
 deep in my dead heart,
Vengeance oozes from my being, I wish to
 rend the invaders apart.

Forced to look back from this side of death it
 seems transparently clear,
that such evil acts and inhuman ways should
 not be allowed to steer
the future of your world and its people in
 life's ongoing flux and flood,
You must all resist this deadly blight and shed
 bright hope instead of blood.

Coda

The picket of the Russian embassy is now well into its second year, the protesting group convinced more than ever of the barbarity of Russia's actions, and the obligation to continue this gesture of defiance. We protest for the voiceless: the unnamed people killed in their homes, the women raped and murdered, the children orphaned, the elderly in the razed cities, towns and villages, the peaceful lives disrupted. But we protest also in solidarity with the right of the military forces of Ukraine to fight in defence of their country. Right, decency and democracy are on their side. Putin and the Kremlin's evil must not prevail.

The staff at the embassy are given a constant reminder of their country's completely unjustifiable aggression. At the very least it causes them discomfort and embarrassment. They complain about our presence. Ambassador Filatov has condemned us. Our protest has been covered by media across the world.

We are heartened by the constant gestures of support from passers-by. Our resolve will not weaken. We invite you to join us on the protest and stand in solidarity with Ukraine and its people.

Slava Ukraini!